Dealers
Buying, Selling & Making Money

Also by Stephen Outram…

Books:
Public Speaking: Beyond Fear
Advanced Speaking Concepts
The Wedding Speeches
There's No Sex in Golf
Life Before

Blog & Articles:
stephenoutram.com

Dealers
Buying, Selling & Making Money

By Stephen Outram

Foreword by Steven Bowman

Disclaimer: This product is designed to provide information and motivation to readers. It is sold with the understanding that the publisher is not engaged to render any type of psychological, legal, or any other kind of professional advice. The content of this product is the sole expression and opinion of its author, and not necessarily that of the publisher. No warranties or guarantees are expressed or implied by the publisher's choice to include any of the content in this product. Neither the publisher nor the author shall be liable for any physical, psychological, emotional, financial, or commercial damages, including, but not limited to, special, incidental, consequential or other damages. Our views and rights are the same: You are responsible for your own choices, actions, and results.

Author: Stephen Outram

Date Published: August 1, 2014

ISBN: 978-0-9802927-5-6

Publisher: What Else is Possible?
PO Box 1770, Broadbeach, QLD. 4218. Australia

© 2014 Stephen Outram. All rights reserved.

This material may not be reproduced, displayed, modified or distributed without the express prior written permission of the copyright holder. For permission, contact www.stephenoutram.com

Stephen Outram

Contents

Foreword *By Steven Bowman*	8
Preface *A Great Treasure Hunt*	10
Thank You! *Wonderful Gifts*	13
What's in this Book? *A Must-Read*	14
Introduction *Making Things Move*	18
Treasure Hunters *Hunters of Treasure*	21
Collectors *An Ancient Profession*	33
Bargainers *Getting Out of the Bazaar*	44
Speculators *Contemplate, Consider and Observe*	55
Investors *Putting on the Uniform*	65
Dealers *Movers & Shakers*	77
Epilogue *Final Thoughts*	89

Appendix *Additional, Bonus Material*	91
Gambling *Playing Risky Games*	92
Hoarding *Hidden Treasure*	96
About The Author *Biography*	100
Other Books *By Stephen Outram*	102

Foreword

By Steven Bowman

"What if having an awareness of the different styles or personas that people adopt, would assist you in your wheelings and dealings in life?

What if a greater awareness of your own personas that you adopt would assist you in looking at things differently?

I have known Stephen for over 10 years now, and have seen him creating his life and businesses from a space of looking at things from a different point of view and his willingness to try new things in ways others would not consider. This book is yet another example of his different way of looking at the world.

My wife, Chutisa, and I have a global business dealing with many hundreds of senior executives and Directors in corporations each year. Looking at how each person chooses to function, and being aware of how they choose to see the world, and working with those awareness's is what has created our business. This book provides a different way of looking at how people choose to function. The various personas of Treasure Hunter, Collector, Bargainer, Speculator, Investor and Dealer all have implications for how we choose to interact with the world around us, and greater insight into how we choose to be in any situation.

When you read this book, you will ask yourself all sorts of questions like, "Hmm, I wonder where I am being that?" or "Interesting. How can I use that to my advantage?" If no questions come to my mind, Stephen has provided some very interesting questions throughout the book to jog you into some self reflection.

Congratulations Stephen on sharing your unique way of viewing the world in a way that others may find beneficial and interesting.

Steven Bowman
Master of Associated Management.
Managing Director of 'Conscious Governance' and 'No More Business As Usual.' Best selling author, *Prosperity Consciousness, Leading From the Edge of Possibility (No More Business As Usual)*.

www.conscious-governance.com

Stephen Outram

Preface

A Great Treasure Hunt

In 2012 I was invited to go antique shopping with author Gary Douglas, Dr. Claudia Cano, jeweler Shari Louise Wright and her husband Roy; we were in Brisbane, Australia. The shopping trip included research that we were doing prior to opening a new antique store, The Antique Guild, in the city. Gary was an experienced antique dealer and it turned out to be wonderfully instructive for me as I observed Gary working, no, playing in a field that he clearly enjoys.

Gary was very generous and included us all in his dealings as we explored some of Brisbane's most interesting places. It was a great day for me and piqued my own interest in antiques and its business. And it ushered in the gentle whisperings of an idea and was where the first character, "Dealer" showed up.

Some months later I heard about an event called Rocky Swap, held in the City of Rockhampton, Queensland and boasting one thousand stalls, including antiques and collectables; a "treasure hunter's paradise" the advertising read. Rockhampton is a six hour drive from where I was living at the time and at 4:00am one Saturday morning, my friend Liam Phillips and I jumped into his car and roared off to Rocky.

We arrived at Rocky Swap around 10:00am and it was huge! And although we walked around it all day, we only purchased two small sterling silver items. It was on the long drive home that Liam and I had a conversation during which two other treasures introduced themselves, "Treasure Hunter" and "Collector."

I had become very interested in antiques and created a class; an immersive workshop called *Making Money with Antiques*. The idea was to take a group of people to a large fair held in Nambour called *Collectorama*, give them tools and send them out on tasks, where they interacted with the various stall holders.

We met for a working breakfast in a local coffee shop, then went to the fair. During the day I went with the various participant groups, learned a lot more about Collector and met "Bargainer" at one of the stalls. The day culminated with a show-and-tell, with everyone dwarfed under a huge Morton Bay fig tree like excited elves in the forest.

Following several of these workshops I had enough information to begin writing this book and during that process "Investor" and "Speculator" let me know they would like to be included too.

It's interesting to note that even though Dealer was the first to show up, it wasn't until I had explored and written up all of the others that the full scope of this extraordinary character came into my awareness. I recall coming home late one afternoon, after writing Dealer's chapter at my favorite coffee shop, and describing to

Simone what I had realized.

It reminds me, that if you wait to have *all* of the information before starting, then it's unlikely you will start at all. For a treasure hunter like me, much is revealed during the hunt itself; that's the real adventure and one that I'm very glad to have chosen.

Warm Regards,
Stephen Outram

Thank You!

Wonderful Gifts

My thanks and gratitude particularly to the following people who have contributed to this book, and me.

To Steven Bowman for your friendship, generosity and for writing an insightful and engaging 'Foreword.'

Dr. Claudia Cano, Shari and Roy Wright for being an amazing gift in this adventure.

Simone Phillips for editing, proofreading, and hearing. Your generosity, warmth and willing contribution is a wonderful gift to me.

To my family: Trevor, Molly and Karen for without you many things would have not been possible.

Gary Douglas for taking me antique shopping; dealing me many new hands, igniting a spark and for being a consummate dealer.

Liam Phillips for being part of a memorable hunt that took us to Rocky Swap, and creating a fun day where I found wonderful treasure. I hope that you did too.

The participants of all *Making Money with Antiques* workshops for your willingness to show up, ask questions and have fun.

Stephen Outram

What's in this Book?

A Must-Read

This section is an overview on how the chapters are designed to provide you a broad yet comprehensive cross-section of information. My target in writing is that the more you read, the clearer your sense of how you embody particular characteristics will become. And that you may have greater insight about how you function in the world; from there you can make some different choices … I know that I did.

Each of the main chapters has a similar format and following is a brief outline of each:

The Beginning

A varied and interesting conversation about the featured character, including quotes and other relevant commentary or contributory information.

Literally

Looking at the makeup of a word; its etymology reveals information that is not always clear (often hidden) from a contemporary perspective. Every word is a precise arrangement; a formula of characters designed for a specific purpose. As time goes by, that purpose and its effect can become obfuscated. We need to be clear about what we say and be aware of the effect of what we say or think. Words contribute to what we create; their incorrect use may result in confusing results.

History

Words and their usage have a lineage; a family tree, which can provide valuable insight into their evolution over time. It's interesting to note that even though a word's perceived meaning or its usage changes over the years, its core idea remains. A word's history provides a richer context and greater understanding.

> "The context of a piece of language ... is its surrounding environment. But this can include as little as the articulatory movements immediately before and after it, or as much as the whole universe, with its past and future."— Paul Werth, from *Text Worlds: Representing Conceptual Space in Discourse*.

Stories

Each chapter contains three to four real-life stories, offered as contextual examples of a particular persona or their characteristics.

Taking Advantage

While this may be useful information in manipulating others, I hope it will be more valuable to you in grasping:

1. How *you* can be manipulated by others.

2. That *you* may be using a core strength; a capacity against yourself and to your disadvantage.

Being Advantage

Each character has talents and abilities that can be quite extraordinary. By having an awareness of these capacities and acknowledging where they apply to you, means you can begin to access and use them in ways that you may not have considered possible before.

Quiz

This provides an engaging and enjoyable way to review some of the key concepts presented in each chapter.

Self Reflection

Sometimes new information about yourself can be exciting or challenging and often you will want to know more. Perhaps something will come up for you while reading a chapter and you know there is more but can't quite reach it; access it…questions can provide awareness.

> "We have been taught that we are supposed to have the right answer; our tendency is to look to get the answer from every question we ask as though getting the answer is the job. What we are looking for is to get "awareness" from the question, not answer; we are looking for the awareness that will give us a greater awareness."—Gary Douglas, founder of Access Consciousness.

Ask yourself the questions provided and, as Gary Douglas describes, allow the awareness of what you are asking to reveal itself, without demanding an immediate answer. You may just find that you already *know* way more than you realize.

Appendix

There are two additional, *bonus* chapters in the Appendix. While these do not describe new characters, they may go some way to explain the more extreme actions our characters can take, in certain situations.

Introduction

Making Things Move

This book began with a simple but powerful realization, there are people in the world that make things move! Are you one of them?

Then that idea grew to include: people in the world that make things stuck and, on to people who see things that are stuck and don't do anything to unstick them. I could say more but you get the idea.

Now, the first group of people often make money, while the other people spend all of their money. That got my attention. How about you? Which one would you like to be?

You see, it takes a lot of energy to hold something stuck (think of holding a stretched rubber band), but very little energy to move it (let go). Yet many people will hold on tight for as long as they can, or not do anything that might create a change.

The people who make things move can get paid very well by the people who can't. And there's more … the people who move things create movement (obviously), activity, change, evolution, liveliness, enterprise, flow … they invigorate the world and stir up new possibilities, for themselves and for others.

That's what this book is about; discovering if you are stuck and what it will take to get unstuck and move more dynamically than ever before (did you let go of that rubber band yet?). And to begin making money, or at least a lot more than you did while you were stuck!

Did you know that the person holding the rubber band doesn't realize they are stuck; they don't know how to let go; they think that's all there is; it's what they do; they hold on tight for as long as they can. They need someone to assist them to move. Is that someone you?

Imagine if everyone in the world was stuck; holding on tight and unaware that anything else is possible, then nothing new or different would be created. It would be like a huge global traffic jam; eventually all the vehicles would run out of gas and that would be that! Does that seem like much fun?

People that make things move, and can make money, are called Dealers. Are you one? Would you like to be?

Well, first you need to discover if you are stuck and don't know it. Are you? The good news is that as you become more aware of what's sticking you and choose to let go of it, then you get to have more movement. With more movement you will find there are different choices available and more to create with; more money to make and more fun to have too.

Where do you start?

In the upcoming pages are five chapters presenting five familiar but sticky characters. You may already know one or two of them well. If you are being one of them, then you may be stuck and don't know it. If you get to know them all, and use them to advantage, then you can embrace number six.

Number six is the one that makes things move; number six can make lots of money; number six is Dealer.

And remember, you need them all to be a Dealer; so skipping to the back of the book to get the answer won't work.

The world needs, no, is demanding people who can make things move to step up. The rewards are incredibly high, in ways you cannot imagine yet. Will you get yourself unstuck and assist others?

We need more people making things move. We need you. Will you deal?

Treasure Hunters

Hunters of Treasure

It is the hunt and rarely the treasure that is of prime interest to treasure hunters.

When the phrase 'treasure hunter' is reversed, it reveals much more accurately the energy that these people function from. "Hunters of Treasure" brings into focus the key influential activity, which is hunting. This is even clearer when using the verb *treasure* hunting, where treasure (v.) means figuratively, to "regard as precious." Hunting is regarded as precious.

> "One does not hunt in order to kill; on the contrary, one kills in order to have hunted…
> If one were to present the sportsman with the death of the animal as a gift he would refuse it. What he is after is having to win it, to conquer the surly brute through his own effort and skill with all the extras that this carries with it: the immersion in the countryside, the healthfulness of the exercise, the distraction from his job."— Jose Ortega y Gasset, Philosopher, *Meditations on Hunting.*

The treasure itself can be many different things; thousands of years ago it may have been a prime beast that would feed the tribe, perhaps a handful of salt or a fine horse; today it may be an antique piece of jewelry, fine art, the latest smart phone or money. Treasure is very subjective to the moods of the time and an individual's interests.

Treasure hunters fall into two main categories:

1. Those seeking to find treasure that they lost or secreted-away (perhaps in another lifetime).

2. Those seeking to find someone else's treasure, lost or otherwise.

Seeking Hidden Treasure

In many civilizations, during times of political trouble or war, people would hide their wealth by burying it in the ground.

> "Because of the turmoil of the 3rd Century and precisely the dangers we face today as government goes after citizens hunting down their wealth to confiscate...Hoards [of roman coins] from the 3rd Century are far more common. Pots with up to 50,000 coins have been discovered." Martin Armstrong, "Roman Coins"

In 2012, a hoard of Roman gold coins valued at over £100,000 was found by a novice English Treasure Hunter, Wesley Carrington. He was using a basic metal detector and located the hoard buried in woods near St. Albans, Hertfordshire. Commenting on the find Julian Watters, Liaison Officer for Hertfordshire & Bedfordshire said, "It is something you dream of as a child finding buried treasure."

If you are open to the idea of having lived in other lifetimes, is it possible that some people are driven to recover their previously hidden wealth?

Another contemporary example of hunting is the 2010 TV show called *Auction Hunters*, which features two men (Allen Haff and Clinton "Ton" Jones) buying abandoned storage containers, hunting amongst the contents and selling the most lucrative and interesting pieces to experts or collectors. They find some amazing things.

Burglars and thieves are in the business of stealing other people's treasure. The Great Train Robbery, an infamous 1963 event, became world news and was made into a documented film of the same name. The robbers, lead by Bruce Reynolds, got away with over £2.6 million heisted from a UK Royal Mail train. Most of the gang were later caught and jailed, though Ronald "Ronnie" Biggs escaped and fled to Brazil.

Romantically portrayed in many movies, documentaries and reported in the media; treasure hunters will dig for buried treasure based, often, on the feeblest of information. They dream of pushing their shovel into the earth to feel it jar as the blade strikes something substantial. And then, one shovel-full at a time, uncovering a hoard of fabulous, glittering wealth; a treasure.

> "After 12 days of digging for gold on the basis of a seer's dream, archaeological excavations have not found any gold trace yet in the bizarre hunt for 1,000 tonnes of the yellow metal supposed to

> be buried under the ruins of a 19th century fort in Unnao in Uttar Pradesh."—Reported in The Times of India, October 2013

> "Oak Island [Nova Scotia] is noted as the location of the so-called Money Pit and the site of over 200 years of treasure hunting."— Heather Whipps, For Sale: Island with Mysterious Money Pit

As children, we are taught the thrill of the hunt during birthday parties or Easter egg treasure hunts. Those who are quick to untangle the clues, decipher a cryptic map or run faster than the others, might be first to find the prize and seize it!

> "There comes a time in every rightly constructed boy's life that he has a raging desire to go somewhere and dig for hidden treasure."—Mark Twain

Many people report experiencing the highly excited state known as "adrenaline rush" while hunting.

> "Treasure hunting is an art, a science and an adrenalin rush all rolled into one."—W C Jameson, Professional Treasure Hunter and author of *Buried Treasures of America*

> "… the [Paris] Louvre transforms from a vast, somewhat overwhelming art museum into an adrenalin-pumping hunting ground."—Excerpt from "Treasure Hunts at the Louvre," The Boston Globe, 2013

According to an article on Fit Day, the thrill of the

adrenaline rush is the exciting, pleasurable effect produced when the adrenal glands dump a large dose of adrenaline into the bloodstream.

> "Your heart rate increases, pleasure-giving endorphins are released by the pituitary gland and your breathing rate ramps up. The result of all this extra oxygen, energy and hormones is the adrenaline high, a euphoric feeling that can last for hours."—fitday.com

Treasure hunters are persistent; they are skilled puzzle solvers, searching patiently for clues. Their target is to find those elusive threads that seem tantalizingly real and to follow them as far as they go; perhaps over many lifetimes. Treasure hunters are not really interested in finding the treasure, they like hunting and the hunt.

Literally

The Old English word (early 12th Century) huntian means to "chase game, to seize or capture." And in the more general sense "to search diligently." Associated with Native Americans, "Happy hunting-grounds" is regarded as afterlife paradise.

The Hunt was described, circa 1570, as "body of persons associated for the purpose of hunting."

History

The men of a primitive tribe would search diligently for game, pursue it (the hunt) and hopefully make a kill. Returning to the tribe with game was cause for great celebration. Those directly involved in the kill were heroes and honoured with the choice meats and high status.

The rewards were short-lived as hunters needed to constantly affirm their potency and skill with each new hunt. As they grew less able, their standing in the tribe changed and some became story tellers, reliving their glory days with those who would listen.

It was a big deal to find the treasure and bring it home, for some, even worth dying for. Those who died in great hunts became legends, told about in stories around the campfire, and their contribution to the tribe's sense of itself passed down through the generations.

Today, in the more developed countries hunting for food is done in air conditioned grocery stores, though hunting as a sport is very popular. The equipment used is sophisticated, accurate and deadly, and provides a big advantage to the hunter. Even where some sports people hunt with bow and arrows, the weapon technology is far superior to any of old.

Stories

A secondhand story ...
My friend is always exploring second-hand and charity shops. He makes regular visits to antique and bric-a-brac stores; loves car boot sales, garage sales and the like. Occasionally he will buy, though this is rare.

I recall when he found a treasure - a string of natural graduated pearls with sterling silver clasp, hallmarked c1920 and priced at $125. My friend went back to the store several times and even joked with the shop keeper, "Look after my pearls." He knew it was a treasure but didn't buy it.

He would have been happy for someone he knew to purchase the pearls, on his recommendation; it would've been important to him that they knew he had found the treasure.

Why would my friend not have bought the treasure and sold it on for a profit, give it as a gift or kept the pearls for himself? The answer is simple; he is a hunter. His interest is the hunt for treasure and once a treasure is found his job is done.

An intellectual story…
Someone else that I know is highly intellectual and actually, quite brilliant. Let's call him John.

John has the capacity to grasp whole concepts; all of the parts at the same time. He has a notebook full of great ideas, based on his awareness and observations of the world. Each idea is conceptualized, explored and written up. There are some ideas that he has researched and expanded to create a credible prospectus document, suitable for investors.

The interesting thing is that he will give these away to someone else rather than develop them himself. Why would he do that?

For John, each idea is an intellectual treasure that he has hunted for and found. He describes these in words, in his notebook, so that others may know them too. Once an idea is explored and written up, he is done with it and moves on to the next treasure that is waiting patiently to be discovered.

As a hunter of intellectual treasure, John's notebook is the only record of his discoveries. While it may be highly-valuable for the concepts and innovation contained within its pages, to John... it is practically worthless.

A romantic story ...
In the popular movie 'Titanic,' treasure hunters dive on the ancient shipwreck in hope of finding treasure. They discover the picture of a beautiful woman, naked except for the fabulous jewel she wears. 'Star of the Ocean' is known to them and they search to find its wearer.

By good fortune or luck they find Rose; one of the few people to survive Titanic and reach the Americas. Our treasure hunters contact her and invite the now grandmother to their ship; to return to the Titanic and tell her story. She accepts.

Rose unfolds a romantic tale, we now know from the movie, of her love-affair and tragic loss of a young adventurer called Jack. She, of high birth meets chivalric Jack on-board and so begins an unlikely but passionate romance.

When Titanic strikes an iceberg and sinks, Jack uses all his skill and finally sacrifices his own life to ensure that Rose survives. When a lifeboat finally plucks Rose out of the chill Atlantic, Jack's frozen body slips beneath the waves to rejoin the great ship.

Late one evening Grandmother Rose, having finished telling her story to the treasure hunters, secretly drops the fabulous Star of the Ocean into a cold Atlantic and returns it to Titanic…and her beloved Jack.

The fabulous jewel and everything it represents becomes, once again, a treasure hunter's dream. And perhaps Rose, in some future life, will try to reclaim all that she secreted-away within Titanic. A hunter looking for a lost treasure that calls to her beyond the waves… and time.

Taking Advantage

Sell Treasure Hunters clues, maps, stories of legend and other tantalizing information. Sell them the treasure map and not the treasure. Connect them with probabilities, possibilities and large worthy concepts such as solving mysterious legends, finding the cure for disease or world changing events (think of the 1984 adventure film *Romancing the Stone*, Mapping the Human Genome, 2003 or changing the world).

Treasure Hunters like to figure it out themselves, they like the hunt. Even hunting for a map is preferable to being given the map. Give these people research projects, mysteries and puzzles, for example, whenever I require new functionality for my website I ask someone I know, who joyfully heads off into the Internet and returns sometime later with the perfect thing. I have no idea how she does it, but it works.

Make sure to praise and acknowledge treasure hunters for their skill with hunting. Be grateful for the treasure they bring you and, reward the hunt. Sometimes all the reward that is required is for you to ask them questions and to sit and listen; be enthralled by their tale as they recount and celebrate the great adventure.

Buy from Treasure Hunters the treasure; after they have found it and the celebration is done; then it has little value to them. They like to hunt...right?

Being Advantage

Treasure hunters can be brilliant problem solvers; they are observant, perceptive and adaptable.

Treasure hunters can have keen tracking abilities, are persistent and pay attention to detail; they see what others do not. They can be highly perceptive and skilled at piecing together clues and different data that may confuse others less able. They are great researchers and explorers of information that can contribute to revealing a previously mysterious bigger picture.

Treasure Hunters are also able to adapt quickly to changing circumstances. Rarely, if ever, do they give up, even when the map has been totally destroyed and the trail seems lost; like bloodhounds they will search far and wide to find a single tantalizing gossamer thread that may point the way.

> "Till the gossamer thread you fling catch somewhere, O, my soul."— Walt Whitman, from "A Noiseless Patient Spider"

Quiz

Use the following questions to review what you recall about this chapter:

1. What treasure is the most precious to Treasure Hunters?

2. What are the two main categories of Treasure Hunters?

3. How are children taught to hunt for treasure?

4. What is the term used to describe caches of roman coins, found buried in the ground?

5. What is the "rush" Treasure Hunters enjoy while hunting?

6. What role do older hunters play in primitive tribes?

7. List three ways you can take advantage of Treasure Hunters.

8. Describe three skills treasure hunters have.

Self Reflection

In reading the previous sections you may have identified certain characteristics that you have. Use the following questions to access greater awareness and clarity in this area:

- How long have you been hunting for all the treasure that once was yours?

- How far into the future are you searching for treasure that you have not yet even created?

- What treasure was stolen from you that you have vowed to find and take back, even if it takes you forever?

- Are you preoccupied with finding someone else's treasure rather than creating your own?

- What will it take for you to use everything that you know about hunting, to find, value and enjoy the treasure called "You?"

- What do you know about treasure hunting that you can now use to advantage?

Collectors

An Ancient Profession

Collectors place much greater value on their incomplete group of items than they do on a group that is finished.

The word collector is largely misunderstood. Collector is a long-lived profession that has been in existence since the invention of taxes. These were high-level jobs, working for Pharaohs, Caesars and Kings though it is noted in ancient records that tax collectors were not well liked and viewed as despicable.

> "No generation has ever loved those who carry out civil taxation, but what made these men so "despicable?"— Kyle Pope, from *Tax Collectors and Sinners*

In ancient Egypt, Scribes were educated to read and write, measure, record and collect taxes from farmers and other business, though perhaps these days it is accountants that work the numbers. Times have changed (though people's opinions may not) and today, tax collection is handled less personally, often digitally. Some governments with a Goods & Services Tax (GST, VAT) in place have covertly and cleverly engaged the private sector; business to collect taxes for them.

> "... you are required to collect GST tax from your customers for the goods and services rendered by you and then pay the tax collected to tax authorities." —Janus Corporate Solutions, from Singapore Goods and Services Tax (GST) Guide

The contemporary meaning given to collector is a person whose hobby is collecting such things as plates, stamps, paintings, Tupperware® or if they are like Elizabeth Taylor…husbands. Today, all manner of items are collected, regardless of their value.

A further misconception is the generalization that a collection is a group of related objects. This is incorrect, "collection" is the *action* of a collector.

The hobby collector is focused on gathering related items together and their goal is to never-complete the set. This makes sense because what they are really doing, albeit unconsciously, is doing the real job of a collector, they are employed in the action of collection.

Once a group of items is completed, a collector can no longer collect for it (they can no longer do their job). So, they will use various techniques to achieve their real goal of never-completing the group they are working on and therefore be able to continue collecting.

A collector may try to prolong their work, for example, by:

- Seeking better pieces to swap-in for lesser ones in the group
- Beginning projects that may take more than one

lifetime

- Collecting very rare objects and thereby reducing the risk of actually acquiring all of the necessary pieces
- Rejecting items because they are just not good enough
- Constantly researching, revising and updating the information in a book project and never getting it finished (collectors of information)
- Selling a large incomplete project in a grand way

The key thing to know about collectors is, they like collecting and are not interested in completing the group. They will pretend that they are creating a valuable product to sell and make money with, but this is the justification they use to continue doing their work.

A group of objects can become vastly more desirable and valuable when complete, yet collectors rarely enjoy this financial benefit, while pretending they are collecting to make money. The thrill of completing a group quickly fades when collectors realize their work is done. For a collector, the thrill is really in the action of collecting.

Collectors, even those in business, are rarely willing to make money. They will often call their activity a hobby as reason and justification for losing money.

A collector may say, "I do this because I love it; the

money is not important."

There is nothing wrong with this point of view. There is no rule that says you have to make money. Collecting can be done purely for the fun of it. But be aware, if you are not getting the financial results you would like from collecting, ask yourself, "Have I created a hobby designed to lose money?"

Literally

You will find "lect" contained in words such as: intellect, election, lecture, recollect and collect. Lect seems to contribute this "gathering" energy to words that it is used with.

The word collect, with its prefix co meaning "together" coupled with lect from the Latin legere "to gather" gives us the meaning "to gather together."

History

Taxes, in ancient Egypt, were collected and recorded by scribes. In Rome, publicans collected for their Caesars. During the late 14th Century, collector was the unpopular "gatherer of taxes," working for the King. Of similar ilk, debt collectors are disliked and feared to this very day.

> In how many lifetimes have collectors worked as tax or debt collectors and are still doing that job (and probably not being paid) in this lifetime?

From the 1530s, money gathered for religious or charitable purposes became known as "collection" and a trusted person was appointed to do that job.

> How many churches, religions and charitable organizations have collectors worked for, passing around the collection bowl?

Collectable, a word from the late 1800s relates to those items that are valued by collectors i.e. "things worth collecting." An object or item that is considered collectable is sought-after and highly prized by collectors of that particular genre.

Today, digital information or data is collected. Every day, There are 1000s of gigabytes (GB) of data collected and stored. In Australia, every bank transaction is recorded and stored; most of them will never be looked at or used. In the USA, the National Security Agency (NSA) has been in the news for covertly collecting all types of communications data: emails, texts, phone calls, etc. A growing business trend includes those people who can make sense of all the data and extract something useful.

Stories

An antique story ...
I took a group of class participants to "Collectorama," which is an antiques and collectables fair held in Nambour, Australia. It features over 500 exhibits covering a huge range of categories. It's a great event that was the venue for my full-day class entitled "Making Money with Antiques."

Browsing with two participants, Max and Natasha, we stopped at a table featuring ceramic and pottery objects and I asked the stall owner what her favorite piece was. She looked around and glanced over all the items several times, taking quite a long time to answer. Finally, she gestured vaguely to her right and said, "I like the Koala salt and pepper shakers." Later, I spoke to my participants and asked what they got from that. We discussed that this lady was a collector who dearly loved every piece on the table; it was difficult to decide on her favorite.

When you are dealing with a collector, they don't really want to sell anything; they are there to proudly display their group. There is little possibility of negotiation, barter or better prices because collectors collect; they don't like breaking up their group…even to make money.

While some collectors will complete a group and create a valuable product, for many, money is rarely part of the computation.

A historical story …
The British Museum in London was originally created from the will of the physician, naturalist and collector, Sir Hans Sloane (1660–1753).

Sloane collected more than 71,000 objects, over his lifetime, which he wanted to be preserved intact after his death. So, he bequeathed the whole collection to King George II for the nation, in return for a payment of £20,000 to his heirs.

The gift was accepted and on June 7, 1753 by an Act of Parliament, which established the British Museum.

The founding collections largely consisted of books, manuscripts and natural specimens with some antiquities (including coins and medals, prints and drawings) and ethnographic material.

Note that Sloane's greatest desire was to have his collection "preserved intact after his death." In bequeathing his collection to the nation he was able to ensure that his life's work would be kept together for a very long time. He received not one penny, for the 71,000 objects, as payment went directly to his heirs.

A certifiable story …
Someone I know always seems to be attending courses. They are one of the most qualified people I've met, with certificates for this, that and the other. If they framed all their certificates and hung them, they would fill a whole wall.

Whenever a new course comes along they are very enthusiastic; talking about the new business to be created or extra clientele that they will have from this new skill. And of course they would like me to go along as well, as they can see how it will benefit me and my business. They go and do the class, get the paperwork and then put it in the drawer; never to be seen again. A month or so later, they are off doing another course.

Collectors of certificates, qualifications and awards can be caught-up in the *doing of courses*, rather than what they can create beyond that. Maybe they just like being certifiable?

Taking Advantage

Collectors place high value on that which is not-yet a part of their incomplete group, and also on items that will add-to their group. They do not value a completed group. Sell collectors objects and items, that they value and desire, as something to expand or improve their group. Collectors will pay well for objects they value and desire.

Ask a collector questions to become aware if they are protective or possessive of the items they have. Get them talking about collecting and perceive their energy; does it change and become more intense when they engage in their passion?

Use questions like:

- How long have you been collecting these [items]?
- What is your very favorite piece?
- What is the history of these [items]?

Never pickup an object without permission or unless it is passed to you by the collector; always point and show respect. Do not ask them where or how they get their stuff. This will be considered highly suspicious (akin to industrial espionage) and they will shut down.

Be genuinely interested in their field. Ask questions, create conversation, act dumb, learn and receive the information you require. You might be amazed at how willing collectors are to talk about their subject, once they connect with you.

Engage collectors in ideas that can lead to new genres to collect, items that are collectable or will be in the future and facilitate the beginnings of a new collection.

Buy or offer to sell for them the completed group that they have lost interest in and that have little value for them. Certain businesses, for example, auction houses, antique dealers and brokers provide an outlet for Collectors who may discount groups that no longer have value to them.

Be aware that collectors, who are actively collecting for their group, do not really want to sell any item. You may pay a high price for an item that they currently consider a valuable part of a group.

Being Advantage

Collectors can be tenacious, patient and caring. These are qualities they bring to everything they do.

Tenacious is being firm, steadfast, someone who can hold the line. People being tenacious are those you can rely on and are unlikely to break down in a tense situation or negotiation.

> "Tenacity is the quality of being tenacious. It means the ability to be persistent in maintaining, adhering to or seeking something valued or desired."—Bruce Elkin, Author

> "Let me tell you the secret that has led me to my goal: my strength lies solely in my tenacity."—Louis Pasteur, Chemist

Patient is about "enduring without complaint." Someone who will wait until the moment is right before taking action.

> "Patience is power. Patience is not an absence of action; rather it is timing, it waits on the right time to act, for the right principles and in the right way."—Fulton J. Sheen, Bishop

"I am extraordinarily patient, provided I get my own way in the end."—Margaret Thatcher, U.K. Prime Minister from 1979-1990

Caring is the desire and appropriate action ensuring that something or someone has what they require. It may include taking-care-of as a duty of care, though in a greater sense caring can be allowing someone to make their own, albeit unwise, choices.

"Caring is total allowance of what people are choosing. If people are choosing what they truly would like to have as their lives, that's their choice, even if it's dying."—Gary Douglas, Author

"If you truly care for them, then you want them to be who they are; that was why you liked them in the first place."—Terry Goodkind, Author

Quiz

Use the following questions to review what you recall about this chapter:

1. What is the action of a collector?

2. What techniques do collectors use to prolong collection?

3. Why are collectors rarely interested in making money?

4. Can you barter with a collector and get a great deal?

5. What are some of the qualities of a collector?

6. Name two ways you can take advantage of a collector.

Self Reflection

In reading the previous sections you may have identified certain characteristics that you have. Use the following questions to access greater awareness and clarity in this area:

- How many lifetimes have you been a collector, tax collector or debt collector and been hated, rejected, reviled and feared; and how many times have you been beaten, injured or killed doing this job?

- What secret decisions have you made about the long-lived and ancient profession of Collector, to ensure that no one would know you as that…ever again?

- Are you still trying to do your job while keeping it hidden?

- Have you designed a hobby that is a highly efficient way to lose money?

- What stupidity are you using to create lack-of-money and losing-money, as a collector?

- How many collections have you begun, in other lifetimes that you are still trying to finish?

- What do you really know about Collector that you can now use to your advantage?

Stephen Outram

Bargainers

Getting Out of the Bazaar

Bargainers can become consumed by their bargaining and forget to negotiate a real deal and make some money.

Bargainers love to bargain. It is often an integral part of any interaction they participate in. It is the interaction, the joust, or haggling to agree (or not) the value of the item or service that is of interest. If someone will not bargain with them, they may not be willing to buy or sell.

Bargaining is the *action* of bargainers and once a price is agreed, their job is done. Handing over, or taking the money or item is secondary; an after-action.

Auctions cleverly manipulate bargainers, by setting them against each other in a bidding competition that is controlled by a single auctioneer. The desire of bargainers to win or not-lose is stimulated. The system of bidder's cards works to identify and force bargainers to hand over their money, especially when they have been *overly enthusiastic* about bargaining and may be having second thoughts.

> "When someone places a bid, he, in essence, believes the item is already his. Thus, when someone outbids him…the original bidder

is more prone to thinking that the second bidder has stolen that item away from him. This intrinsic feeling of ownership that results in placing a bid on an item causes serious bidders to become emotionally rooted—they are offended by those who out-bid them, and they furiously seek to claim what they have already identified as theirs. Pride (to win and to not back out), also comes in to play, especially because bidder history is made very transparent and public on online auction sites like eBay. Winning is a big deal, and losing is shameful."—Cornell University, excerpt from *Bidder Psychology*.

A 2008 study[1] by Gill and Thanassoulis revealed four key features of bargaining:

1. Bargaining involves actively requesting a seller to lower the price

2. Not everyone will bargain

3. Some people bargain with more than one seller

4. Some bargainers do better than others

We can see that bargaining is an activity; it is the action of bargainers. Without one person making an offer and another person making a counter-offer there is no action. A strong tactic is to play one seller off against others and conversely, to pit multiple buyers

---

1   "The Impact of Bargaining on Markets with Price Takers: Too Many Bargainers Spoil The Broth." by David Gill, U of Southampton & John Thanassoulis, U of Oxford.

against each other (as in an auction). In addition, that people can use bargaining for or against themselves; to advantage or disadvantage. More on that later.

> "In many auctions, the most irrational person wins."—Seth Goden, from The Magic of Auctions.

A useful observation in the study is that the list price is viewed as an upper bound for bargainers, "… the lower the list price the lower the prices which have to be offered by bargainers," which is why sellers often pad the list price to have room to manoeuvre.

Negotiators
Bargaining is related to negotiating, though there is a big difference. Negotiators work towards an outcome; they know that there will be agreement and their job is about establishing the *terms* of that agreement. Take, for example, a trade union negotiating with a business about higher wages for workers; neither want the business to close or the workers to lose their jobs, so they will negotiate the terms that will allow an agreement to be reached.

Pressure may be applied to the business in the form of workers striking but at the same time, striking pressures the workers as they receive no pay. Eventually the matter is resolved and the workers return to work and the business continues.

Bargainers can become good negotiators though it requires that they be willing to follow through, beyond bargaining, to strike a deal[2] and conclude their action.

Literally

Bargain and haggle are close relatives, with haggle meaning to "chop away." The origins of the word 'barter' lean towards cheating and deceiving.

My sense of the word bargain is it's a combination of two words, bar and gain. Bar being "a rod or stake used to secure a door" and gain "to earn, profit, trade, win." So, bargain meaning "to secure a profitable trade."

To bargain, as an action, seems to have appeared in the 12th Century meaning "to haggle over the price" and in the mid 14th Century "a business transaction or agreement" was used.

In the late 1800s, the idea of "an article priced for special sale" and "bargain basement" (originally was a basement floor in a store where bargains were displayed) came into use.

History

I will suggest that bargaining has been around as long as humans have been on the planet, but perhaps formalized in early markets or bazaars.

> "**bazaar**, originally, a public market district of a Persian town. From Persia the term spread…The

---

[2] From Latin ferire foedus, literally, the expression meant "to strike an agreement," with "to strike" being taken in the sense of "to solemnly commit oneself to, as if sacrificing an animal [by striking and killing it] to a deity."— Darryl Lyman, author *Dictionary of Animal Words and Phrases*.

bazaar of the ancient Islamic world was vividly described in the folktales of *The Thousand and One Nights*. Located in a distinct quarter of the town, it was bustling and noisy by day in contrast to the quiet residential quarters."— Encyclopedia Britannica

In ancient and some modern markets, bartering was popular as it replaced money as a recognized method of payment. One of the first evidences of bartering is around 6000 BC, when cattle was used as money. The barter system traded all sorts of goods and services, such as weaponry, food, or tea.

The Great Depression[3] is one of the most significant time periods throughout the history of bartering. Money was scarce and people had a difficult time getting what they needed. It allowed people to get food or clothing when they needed to and they were allowed to create accounts with businesses.

Bargaining, barter, haggling and negotiating have all contributed to the way that business has evolved and how we obtain our groceries and other items. Today, it is not widely known that an item's ticket-price is an "offered" price, i.e. the price that it is offered for sale. So shoppers may pay the full ticket price, without bargaining directly with the shopkeeper.

These days, with a global marketplace being facilitated by the Internet and online "eCommerce" shopping,

---

3   "The Great Depression was a severe worldwide economic depression in the decade preceding World War II [that] started in 1930…It was the longest, deepest, and most widespread depression of the 20th century."— Wikipedia

bargaining has become much more indirect as consumers, using a smart phone, can make almost instant price comparisons and simply buy at a better price somewhere else.

Stories

An antique story…
At an antique fair, I visited a stand displaying sterling silver and silver-plated (EPNS) items. The moment I placed my hand on a silver-plated Victorian candle stick holder the attendant said, "I can let you have that for $75 (a 25% discount to the ticket price). It was an impressive reduction.

I immediately knew that he was willing to bargain and moved to the item I was really interested in and asked him questions about it, including "Is this your best price?" Once again, his opening gambit was to offer the item-of-interest at a reduced price. I countered with an offer that was a further 25% reduced and bought the piece. The attendant was delighted with the exchange and I took home a lovely sterling silver bowl purchased for a very good price.

The amount of discount, offered by bargainers, provides information about how far they may be willing to go. A substantial 25% off the ticket price gave me a clue that he had much further to go and I countered with a similar amount.

An automobile story…
Sellers of secondhand automobiles always add around 5-10% to the ticket price, over-and-above their ideal sale price. Why is that? They are preparing to be able to

discount and negotiate the price.

Car buyers know that the price is padded and always ask for the discount. Both buyers and sellers know exactly what is going on, yet play this pretend game of bargaining, so they can feel good about the final deal.

On concluding a deal the seller will boast, "I got my price!" and buyers, "I got him down!" And in that you have an important key, the emotional desire of buyers and sellers to feel that they did well, even if it is an illusion.

A debating story ...
A business partner and friend, Trevor Jones, enjoyed debate. He didn't mind if he was for or against the motion; Trevor could create the case either way. I recall when we were discussing a client who was late in paying our invoice.

At first Trevor sided with me agreeing that the client was in the wrong and then, as if a switch had been flipped, he was defending the client's action (or lack of it). We parleyed back and forth and with each viewpoint I put forward Trevor was able to counter it.

It was extraordinarily constructive because I gained valuable insight into our client's position, based upon Trevor's client-biased input. After a while I changed tactic and simply agreed with everything he said. There was no one to debate with anymore and he responded with something like, "Oh well. Handle it as you see fit."

Trevor was an intellectual bargainer; once there was no one to bargain with, he lost interest in the client. I contacted our lawyers and they hand led the matter.

A wasting time story ...
I needed to buy some suspension parts for my classic car and rather than pay the full retail price, searched through several online forums that I knew of. I found someone who had bought the parts for his car and not fitted them; he had subsequently sold his car and was now looking to sell the spare parts.

I contacted him via the forum and he said that he could let them go for $475. I asked after his best price and he responded with $475. We corresponded some more and I then asked him to provide a quote for shipping; he came back with $40. I offered him $500, including postage. He replied and said $507 would seal the deal. With that I laughed out loud!

In that moment I realized that he was not a bargainer. I had corresponded with him, over the course of two weeks, to negotiate a $7 discount. If I had asked the question, "Will this person bargain with me?" at the start, then I would have known much earlier. The clue I missed was in his first email, "I can let them go for…" He was a collector, with an attachment.

Taking Advantage

True bargainers will often lead with discount. There is an energy they present, which you can come to recognise. Other people, who pretend to be bargainers, always seem false. Perhaps they were told to bargain by a friend but deep down they don't get it or even like it. These people are easy to take advantage or get rid of.

Ask yourself, "Will this person bargain?" you will know.

Bargainers like to bargain, so bargain with them.

Ask bargainers questions to gain information about the item for sale and about them. When you are ready, begin the negotiations. Do not respond to their opening offer until you are fully ready. If you begin, start with a low price and observe their reaction.

When buying from bargainers, play the game and take note of the amount of discount being offered to determine if you are getting close to their best price. The amount of discount often gets smaller as they get closer to their bottom price. Know what your best offer is before you begin and stick with it.

Be willing to walk away and end the negotiation. In so doing you take control, by taking away what bargainers enjoy the most…bargaining.

When selling to bargainers, make sure you have enough on the ticket price, to negotiate. They are much more likely to buy if they get a discount. Know, in advance, what your bottom price is and when you're done then sigh, shake your head and say something like, "Wow! You have me at my bottom price; will you take it?"

When buying from bargainers ask, "Are you flexible with the price?" rather than, "Are you fixed on your price?" Generally, they will say "Yes" to either question—which response would you prefer?

Being Advantage

Bargaining and its cousin negotiating are desirable capacities and skills that are highly valued in industry, business, sales, politics, relationships, etc. Someone who has acknowledged their capacity to negotiate and enhanced it, will work to create a beneficial outcome or know when something is not available and move on.

Employ bargainers to work for your business. They can become excellent negotiators and given some scope to adjust the price, they can make great sales people. Always set the price range so they know exactly where they must stop or have them refer to a higher-level manager for guidance.

Bargainers can be nimble and "think on their feet," be aware of changes in the behavior of the person they are with and knowledgable about the subject being discussed, and its wider market.

Quiz

Use the following questions to review what you recall about this chapter:

1. What is bargaining?

2. How do auctioneers manipulate bargainers?

3. What is the main difference between bargainers and negotiators?

4. What is the emotional desire that is shared by both buyer and seller?

5. What's another term for an intellectual bargainer?

6. When selling to a bargainer, should you have a firm ticket price and stick to it?

7. What's a great question to ask before you begin bargaining with someone?

Self Reflection

In reading the previous sections you may have identified certain characteristics that you have. Use the following questions to access greater awareness and clarity in this area:

1. Where are you using your capacities to bargain, haggle, barter, debate or negotiate against yourself?

2. Are you using ancient barter or bargaining techniques and methods that no longer work?

3. Are you using bargaining to never complete a negotiation and make no money?

4. Where have you judged bargaining, haggling, bartering, debating or negotiating as a bad thing, and refuse to use them to advantage.

5. What emotional desire are you using the create the illusion that you do well with buying and selling?

6. What can you create with bargaining that you have not been aware of or considered possible before?

Speculators

Contemplate, Consider and Observe

Speculators imagine the future in their mind, and can extrapolate outrageous scenarios based on little or no reliable information.

Speculation is the art of contemplation, consideration and observation. Speculators like to look; they are life's voyeurs who rarely take action, the tyre-kickers who waste your time and never buy, people who are neutral, sitting on the fence, but always willing to give you their opinion.

In this present-day, speculation is often misidentified and misapplied as high-risk investment or a risky venture. This is incorrect; there is low-risk with speculation as a true speculator rarely takes action that would incur risk. The risky venture person is more like an entrepreneur, investor or a gambler who is mainly interested in playing games.

It is wild or uncontrolled speculation that may *fuel* someone's propensity to gamble, but it is the gamble that is high-risk; speculation in itself is simply speculation.

The following headline presents a news article reporting on a missing Malaysian Airline flight MH370. The "wild speculation," in this case, did not fuel risky gambling and illustrates that speculation is not gambling; they are different actions.

> "Missing airliner, stolen passports fuel wild speculation."—The Washington Times, March 2014

And another example from RT News:

> "A new photograph from NASA's Mars Curiosity rover appears to showcase a strong artificial light emanating from the planet's surface, igniting speculation that the beacon suggests there is intelligent life on the Red Planet."—RT News, 2014

A speculator is entertained by the interactions of others and they are often "in their head" pondering what they have seen, what it means and what it might become. To speculate, is the *action* of speculators.

In a sense, speculation is about trying to see the future, by forming a theory without firm evidence. But more correctly, the speculative aspect is where the *imagined* future can be exaggerated beyond all probability, in someone's mind, without the risk of challenge. From a simple beginning; a seed, a complex and fantastic fiction can be developed.

> "A wonderful area for speculative academic work is the unknowable. These days religious subjects are in disfavor, but there are still plenty of good topics. The nature of consciousness, the workings of the brain, the origin of aggression, the origin of language, the origin of life on earth, SETI and life on other worlds…this is all great stuff.

Wonderful stuff. You can argue it interminably. But it can't be contradicted, because nobody knows the answer to any of these topics."— Michael Crichton, MD, author

Speculation ends when the unknowable becomes known, when the inevident becomes evident and the imagined becomes real.

Literally

The suffix -ulate is a key part of the word speculate and suggests "small" or possibly "focussed." This can be seen in words such as articulate, "the ability to divide speech into distinct parts." Spec is a root word that forms part of words such as spectacles, inspect, expectation and respect, adding the quality of sight, as in viewing or seeing something in a particular way.

In the late 14th Century, speculate was described as "contemplation, consideration, observation." "Buying and selling in search of profit from rise and fall of market value" is recorded from 1774; with the short form spec being used from 1794.

History

Speculation has largely been connected with failed financial endeavours. Author Charles MacKay describes that in 1711, the directors of the South Sea Company, "imagined they could…carry on their [speculative] schemes for ever" and proposed to the English Parliament that it take on the entire national debt. When its plans were accepted, its stock began to rise dramatically and innumerable other joint stock companies sprang up solely for the purpose of raising shares. One such company described its purpose as:

> "'A company for carrying on an undertaking of great advantage, but nobody to know what it is.' When the man behind that stroke of genius opened his office in Cornhill, he was mobbed by subscribers, and by three o'clock, had sold all his shares and was £2,000 richer. He was philosopher enough to be contented with his venture, and set off the same evening for the Continent. He was never heard of again."— excerpt from *Delusions and the Madness of Crowds* by Charles MacKay, 1841

With such a chequered history, today speculation can be something that is considered a high-risk financial gamble:

> "Speculation involves trading a financial instrument involving high risk, in expectation of significant returns."—The Economic Times

The term is not limited to money and is used in many areas, for example in a scientific sense, to indicate "…early ideas that ares not yet robust enough to be testable, falsifiable or worthy of being a more formal hypothesis."— Wiki Answers

Stories

A building story …
My ex-brother-in-law was a builder and at one point became enchanted with the idea of building a "spec" house. He planned to borrow capital, build an inexpensive house on borrowed land (Builder's Terms allowed him to secure the land with 5% deposit and

then pay the balance at a future date) and then sell it quickly. Once sold, he would then pay for the land and building costs, and pocket a profit. The concept looked good to him and he talked about it incessantly as he imagined every detail.

The spec house was never built and subsequently there was no sale or profit. As a speculator, he completed the entire project in his head. He could contemplate, consider and observe the whole thing without taking a single money-making action.

When someone speculates on a project, rarely, if-ever, will it be completed. The idea, as something to play with, in their head, can become very real to them. An actionless idea, however, will not make money for its creator.

Builders do build houses as their own project, to on-sell. These are often misidentified as "spec." In fact, they are real products that are completed and sold.

A musical story …
A friend expressed interest in buying a guitar that I had and was for sale; it was a nice solid-wood acoustic made by the British luthiers, Tanglewood. Ann was a guest in my home for a few days, before returning home, and she had picked up the instrument several times.

She appeared enthusiastic and talked with me about having a long-held desire to play the guitar. We talked a lot about the instrument, its features and guitars and music in general. I gave her some lessons, she said that she liked the guitar, we discussed a price and the possibility of Ann buying and taking it home with her seemed very real.

Towards the end of her stay Ann's energy changed and she stopped talking about music and playing the guitar. She began to bargain with me on price, pointing to some marks on the hard-case. Just before leaving she told me that the extra luggage fee she would be charged to take it home was too much, and she would not be buying.

Speculation ends when the imagined becomes real. Ann's fantasy of playing guitar and being a musician could no longer be speculated upon, if she actually owned a guitar and was playing it. In order to continue speculating, she could not allow her desire to become reality.

And herein lies a great difficulty for speculators, that of choosing and taking action to begin the realization of their dreams; and then further choices and action to expand what they created with that initial choice.

Speculators will sometimes pretend to take action so it appears that they are being creative; progressive and then quickly destroy it by, for example, returning an object and getting their money back or making excuses. The risk of ending a juicy and long-held speculation can often be too much.

A stolen ideas story…
Actually, not a story this time but several interesting quotes from people, talking about ideas that have gone on to someone else.

> "Too often, when we think of a great idea, we turn to the person closest to us and share it."—

Charmaine McClarie, McClarie Group

"I spoke to someone I considered a really close friend a few months ago about a business plan. My only problem then was capital. She cheered me on and kept on talking about how brilliant a plan it was. A week ago I saw pictures of her company launch on Facebook. I wasn't even invited. I called a few mutual friends and figured she stole my plan. I tried calling her but she didn't pick my calls."—Pink Poppa, Yahoo Answers

"I stole my friend's idea. I'm close to launching a new product that is based on my friend's idea. She decided to work on it originally, but has given up and stopped pursuing it. A few weeks ago, I decided to build it myself. Now I'm getting ready to launch and I'm worried about my friendship. I should tell her, but I'm not sure how to do it."—Anonymous, Ask Meta Filter

Radio: Marconi vs. Tesla. "Marconi experimented with technologies like the Tesla Oscillator to transmit messages over long distances. Tesla initially tolerated Marconi using his work. He is quoted as having said, 'Marconi is a good fellow. Let him continue. He is using seventeen of my patents.' In 1904 the US Patent Office awarded credit for the invention to Marconi. Tesla attempted to sue the Italian, but he didn't have enough financial resources."—Business Careers Guide

"Over a century ago, someone had the idea of

turning a horse carriage into an automobile. Do you remember who that person was? The people we really remember are the ones who took ideas and built on them,"—Richard Gallagher, author

Taking Advantage

Speculators may be indecisive. Sometimes it seems as though they have a committee of people in their body who are discussing, debating or arguing with each other.

Distract speculators, from their minds by asking them questions. It forces them to be present with you and engage. When *you* dominate the conversation with your story, they can drift into their preferred observer role.

Ask speculators what their *view* is, or what they *think* about certain things. They are skilled observers of the world and may provide you with valuable information.

Speculators often enjoy describing their ideas in great detail. Ask them questions and encourage them to share with you what they have in-mind. You may be able to pick up some brilliant ideas to develop as your own. Be aware that while speculators will share their ideas, if you use one, then publicly acknowledge the source. Often, that is all a speculator requires.

Being Advantage

Speculators can be extraordinarily observant and able to grasp a large amount of information and make sense of it. They see things that others do not and can often present a very different perspective on a subject, issue or about a person.

Wild or uncontrollable speculation can lead to

destructive behavior; but speculation as an evolved capacity is highly valuable. A talented speculator in your business, for example, will know all the places where inefficiencies exist and money is being wasted, and can probably contribute suggestions to improve your operations and processes. An observant parent will know when to step in and pull their child out of an escalating or potentially dangerous situation. A considerate friend may be able to assist you with information, about yourself and your life, that you were unaware of.

When you buy into the idea that speculation is high risk and gambling, then you will be less likely to use it to advantage. When you realize what speculation actually is, then you can have a different possibility.

Quiz

Use the following questions to review what you recall about this chapter:

1. What are the three things that spectators like to do?

2. Describe the difference between speculating and gambling.

3. What was it that the South Seas Company proposed to "take on" in 1711?

4. What is a great difficulty for speculators?

5. Do speculators have a good record for completing projects?

6. What technique can you use to distract spectators

from their minds?

Self Reflection

In reading the previous sections you may have identified certain characteristics that you have. Use the following questions to access greater awareness and clarity in this area:

- What are you speculating about, in your head, that entertains you endlessly?
- What have you decided speculation is that it isn't?
- What can be different if *you* acknowledge your speculative capacities, rather than expecting others to acknowledge them for you?
- What will it take for you to be making money speculating, rather than speculating about making money?
- If you valued your ideas higher than you ever thought possible, will others also have to make that leap?
- What speculation can you act upon, right now, that will change your life?
- What have you decided is so extremely speculative and risky, that actually isn't, that you refuse to act upon it?

Investors

Putting on the Uniform

Once invested, investors give up a large portion of their power and money in exchange for being members of the club.

An investor is someone who prefers to buy into someone else's business, project or organization rather than creating their own. In so doing, they take a risk by passing control of their money into the hands, often, of someone or a board of directors that they have never met or know little about.

An investment in public companies, via a Government regulated stockmarket, may not provide much in the way of power, influence or comfort for investors.

> "…shareholder voting rights in public corporations are, indeed, mostly useless. In fact, this has been true at least since 1932…"—Lynn A. Stout, Professor of Corporate and Securities Law at UCLA School of Law

> " Investors believe they are powerless so they accept the consequences of corrupt business practices with barely a peep."—Jack Waymire, from *Are Investors Powerless to Change Wall Street?*

In the true sense of the word, an investor puts on the clothes or uniform (see Literacy) of the organizations that they invest-in; they become a member of the team. Similar behavior is identified in studies of football fans, where supporters pay for membership, buy and wear the club's colors, pay to go to games and can be fanatically loyal even when the team loses year after year after year.

> "To be a fan through the hard times is a way of celebrating your own purity, getting real meaning from being identified as a fan. It's deep in our psychology, this need to establish a commitment to a team…to say, 'I'm a real fan, somebody who is there for the team through good and bad.'"—Eric Simons, *The Secret Lives of Sports Fans*

A key word here is 'support' as investors can loyally support the organization, with their money, labor or donation in the hope that sometime in the future the team will win and they too can be successful.

> "Basking in reflected glory (BIRGing) is a self-serving cognition whereby an individual associates himself with successful others such that another's success becomes their own."—Aronson, Social Psychology

The *action* of investors is investing i.e. putting on the clothes, and being a member of the team is what they are really interested in. Everything else is secondary, including the risk they take to first obtain and then maintain their membership.

While investing is often associated with finance and money, people invest in many things, for example: jobs or careers, clubs, families, education and reputations.

When investing is no longer possible, for example, when a business ceases or a marriage breaks-up, investors will lament their losses, retire to lick their wounds and regroup before they foray into the marketplace once again. Hundreds of years of boom and bust economic cycles, stockmarket bulls and bears, and marriage/divorce rates speaks to the remarkable tenacity, or stupidity, of investors investing.

Investors, both successful and unsuccessful, simply like investing and participate in membership of some of the most diverse and varied clubs on the planet. Without the support of investors, could cultures, societies or even the human race continue to exist?

Literally

The word invest is created by combining two words, in+vest; vest refers to "vestments or clothes" and so together we get "to clothe in, cover, surround."

In relationship to investing, there is a connection with the idea "to cover a bet,"

> "...to place a bet on something that someone else has already put a bet on, in order to cash in on their potential good luck.—Wikipedia

In the late 14th Century, invest referred to "to clothe in the official robes of an office." It wasn't until 1610, in connection with East Indies trading, that the idea of using money to produce profit was first attested. Later, in the mid 1700s, investment was very much about the conversion of money to property in hopes of profit.

History

Clothing or vestments have been around a very long time; early sewing needles found in Russia are dated to about 30,000 BC. While Wikipedia notes that a primary function of clothing is to improve the comfort of the wearer, vestments have been widely used to indicate status and position.

> A robe, "…the name generally given to a class of official costume, especially as worn by certain persons or classes…a garment, of those given by popes and princes to the members of their household or their great officers."Encyclopedia Britannica 1911

Today, clothing is used not only to indicate social status but all manner of job-types and official positions (blue and white collar workers, kings and queens, judges, bishops, etc.). The German sociologist Georg Simmel suggested that fashion only happens when formal societies with class structures exist, and that capitalism created the defensive elite class that used clothing to separate themselves from the lower classes.

An Internet search of "investment" or "vestments" reveals that the cognitive connection with clothing may have been lost in favor of money and finance, but the original behavior is still apparent. The purchase of a corporation's stock or shares or wearing a football club's colors allows people to associate and identify as a group, defined by the company they keep and support.

Stories

A loaning money story …
A few years ago I loaned money to friends, who required it as bond for a rental house. They were both working and the bond would be held in trust, via a government agency, while they were tenants. I figured the risk was handled, fairly well, in that the money was not spent and would be released from trust when they left the house.

We discussed that I would charge interest for the period and they would pay-down the loan monthly. With that we signed an agreement and I handed over the cash. I had made a loan that would return a profit and they got to move into their new home; it seemed like a good outcome for all. I didn't realize at the time but I had invested not in the two friends but in the house.

In the first month one friend, who had gone travelling overseas, didn't make a payment. I contacted him by email and received no reply. Then again, the next month, there was no payment. I sent a stronger email and after some weeks received a reply.

He said that his situation had changed and he was moving out of the house. And when a new tenant was found, to take his place, then that person could settle with me for the loan. Suddenly, I was financing someone that I had never met and had no agreement with. And it seemed that I had become the provider of bond money for this rental house.

Who was in the weakest position, my friend or me? You may have noticed that my friend was now making the rules and changing the deal.

What I learned from this experience:

- You are in control of your money, until you are not.
- You only get to make the rules before you hand over the money; so make them good ones.
- Be clear about what you are investing-in. It may be different than you think it is.
- Someone who is seeking funding, values you based on the money you have available. Once the deal is done, your perceived value drops considerably.
- When you hand over the cash, you may become the least powerful member of a group.

Fortunately for me, even though my friend did relocate, my capital and the interest were eventually paid in full.

A professional story …
Someone I know is a qualified massage therapist, though only does a few paid massages each year. In the past she was much more active with massage being her main business, though today earns her income elsewhere.

To maintain her professional status she joined an official association, which provides her with membership, suitable insurances and satisfies Government requirements so that clients can claim her fees, against their own medical insurer.

In addition, she is required to attend seminars for a

certain number of hours each year, to satisfy continuing professional development requirements and maintain her qualification.

Even though she rarely massages professionally any more, she continues to invest by attending seminars and paying the association's fees.

She has not yet given up wearing the clothes of a professional massage therapist, even though maintaining her professional standing costs her much more than she earns from that work. Investment and being a member is powerful incentive for investors.

A political story…
Clive Palmer was the youngest life-member in Queensland's National Party's (NP) history, at 36 years of age. He was a former party spokesman of the NP and member of its central council, and was made a life-member of the National Liberal Party (NLP) when the two parties merged in 2008.

Palmer resigned his life membership from the NLP in 2012; he had been a member of these organizations since 1974, some 40 years.

> "I resigned because I took the view that political expediency; the welfare of all Australians was more important than staying [member of] an organisation that was only concerned about lobbyists and concerned about money. I think our country is more important than that."— Clive Palmer, MOP, Official Budget Response 2014

In 2013 he formed the Palmer United Party (PUP),

ran as Member for Fairfax, Queensland and went on to became a Member of Parliament. His party is now influential and described as holding the balance of power.

> In his first speech to Parliament Palmer said, "Leadership, not complacency, is our need today." December 2, 2013

I report this story not to endorse PUP, but to illustrate that even someone with Clive Palmer's impressive history and standing in the NLP is powerless, *in his membership*, to affect great change in an organization. In addition, as a successful businessman and one of Australia's richest men, Palmer's substantial donations to the party did not purchase the power to change it either. The successes that he created as leader of his own businesses, did not translate well while he was invested in and supporting someone else's organization.

By resigning from the NLP and leading his own party; his own organization and inviting others to take up membership of PUP and invest, Palmer may become as successful in politics as he is in business.

Taking Advantage

Invite investors to invest in your business or project and be willing to take their money. Investors like to invest, so create attractive investments for them. And remember, once you have the money you are in charge.

Investors tend to prefer larger clubs; business or deals with existing members, so if your venture is small in numbers then the incentives for new members will need to be good. The high risk of investing in startup companies, for example, can be offset by the *chance* of very high rates of return.

Provide investors with a uniform; be it a share certificate, T-shirt or cap, investors will appreciate a shared identity. Communicate the venture's successes and future aspirations and ensure they are BIRGing. If the venture is not performing well then appeal to the loyal fans and ask for their support in difficult times.

> One of the long-term aims of Liverpool Football Club Supporters' Committee is, "To help ensure fans feel their loyalty is valued by Liverpool Football Club."

Network marketing businesses are very good at working with the idea of their people being part of the organization. These businesses specialize in publicly rewarding members at all levels, with grand annual conferences acknowledging high achievers, who then encourage the less successful to do more.

Buy-from or sell-to investors when their sense of club membership is overpowered by a larger influence—fear or greed. The stockmarket, for example, where people invest in many different businesses, is known for a phenomenon called the herd, or herd behaviour.

> "Investors are portrayed as herds that charge into risky ventures without adequate information and appreciation of the risk-reward trade-offs and, at the first sign of trouble, flee to safer havens."— *Herd Behavior in Financial Markets*, International Monetary Fund

At these times investors, en masse, will sell at a loss to

preserve capital or buy at a premium to be part of the action.

Being Advantage

Investors can be fiercely loyal, supporting the organisations that they are members of. It is this loyalty that provides the foundation of many clubs, business and societies around the world; without investors the world would look very different.

They can excel as team players, willing to be part-of and contribute-to the group and its objectives. As managers, investors will be loyal to a business and its leaders, while teaming well with those who work with them.

Investors are tenacious, in the sense that they rarely give up until a situation becomes hopeless or dismemberment is forced upon them.

Many investors are capable of thorough research and investigation as they explore the entity they have an interest in. Once they are satisfied, they act quickly and decisively.

Quiz

Use the following questions to review what you recall about this chapter:

1. What do investors "put on" when they join an organization?

2. What does BIRGing mean?

3. Today, what is the connection that people generally make when asked about investing?

4. What year did Clive Palmer form PUP?

5. What incentives can you offer investors if your venture is small or not strongly supported yet?

6. What are the two larger influences that can affect investors?

7. Investors are sometimes portrayed as having _____ behavior

Self Reflection

In reading the previous sections you may have identified certain characteristics that you have. Use the following questions to access greater awareness and clarity in this area:

- Where are all the places you function as an investor, to your disadvantage?

- What high-risk gamble are you using to ensure your high-rate of no return on your investments?

- How much have you given up or sacrificed to support the clubs and organizations you member?

- Where are you using BIRGing as a poor substitute for the glory you are capable of creating?

- Who have you sold out, in fear or greed, to follow the herd?

- What will you create, beyond your wildest imagining, when you invest in you and your organizations?

- What do you know about investing that you have not ever considered possible?

Dealers

Movers & Shakers

Dealers are people who can make things move; they create marketplaces, facilitate change and transformation and deal us new cards when we are stuck.

Dealers are a rare and unique group of people who are willing to be any or all of the characters, as required, to make a deal that works. While many people can have strengths in one or two areas, dealers employ the capacities of treasure hunters, collectors, bargainers, speculators and investors to advantage.

This requires a high degree of flexibility and an awareness that is holistic in nature "crossing all borders, no boundaries." Rather than being adept in just one area, dealers can swap or combine skill-sets with enviable ease. Dealers are interested in making deals; deals that work and make money or get results. They look at the whole deal very differently than those focussed only on buying or selling.

> "I have never cared what something costs; I care what it's worth."—Ari Emanuel, Talent Agent and co-CEO of William Morris Endeavor

Being aware includes knowing what is possible and what is not. There is an efficiency in the way dealers function and rather than getting involved in long drawn out negotiations that are overly complex or unclear, dealers will walk away. They do not get caught up in the emotional attachment of winning and losing and move on to other deals.

> "Our business is really simple. When you look at a deal and its structure looks like an octopus or spider, just don't do it."—Timothy Sloan, CFO Wells Fargo

Dealers know that their job is to create movement; flow in the market. In fact, it is dealers that create markets. Where, for example, collectors buy-and-hold creating a log jam in the river, and speculators sit on the river bank thinking about the log jam, and investors join a green movement and support the logs being jammed…dealers work to free the jam and move those logs down-river from sellers to buyers. They are facilitators that unblock stuck energies and contribute to the health and vitality of local, domestic and international economies of all sizes.

Dealers understand that the main part of their work is not to buy and sell, but to *connect* buyers and sellers, or to connect those people who want something with that which they desire. They are temporary custodians or stewards pulling together the threads of a deal that will allow an object to get to its new owner or an objective to be realized. Dealers are in the business of collection and distribution; they like to hold all the cards and then deal them out, tantalizing and manipulating winners and losers alike. Dealers like to be in control.

> "'Stop cheating!' the dealer told the card player. 'I'm not!' claimed the player. 'You must be,' said the dealer 'that is not the hand that I dealt you.'"—Anonymous

Dealing or the dealer are terms well known in card games such as Black Jack, offered by many casinos. We find similar characteristics in the dealer of a game as with other dealer-types.

The card dealer gathers all of the cards together and then distributes them out to the players. They take-in money (casino chips) from the losers and pay out to the winners. Dealers facilitate the game and create its flow, and in the process extract commissions that are subtly spun off into their own stack of chips.

Whether it is in a casino, where a dealer represents "the house," a friendly game of Gin Rummy at home with the family or in the business marketplace, dealers facilitate flows of energy that create change and possibility for all participants.

> "Deals are my art form. Other people paint beautifully on canvas or write wonderful poetry. I like making deals, preferably big deals. That's how I get my kicks."—Edward Kochm, former Mayor the City of New York and Author

In their chosen area, dealers are aware of current trends, an item's popularity and market prices. While they are willing to get a bargain, it is not their prime motivation; they are interested in participating and having a share of the deal. They take a holistic view and see the deal as made up of various mutable parts, for example, an item's perceived and actual value, the players and other deal makers. Dealers are aware of all aspects of a particular deal and can manipulate or change the deal as required, or walk away.

Dealers are also aware when a deal is alive or dead.

> "I put in a strong bid. If it's not for sale, it's not for sale."—David Ford, UK Antique Dealer, Secret Dealers TV Show

In the deal, dealers will leave space for the buyer to make money too. They do not function from bartering and squeezing every last drop of blood out of the deal. In this they are generous of spirit and recognise that a deal requires juice; energy to be alive. And even though they may close *this* deal; it is but the beginning of many more as the object or objective moves on.

> "I have found no greater satisfaction than achieving success through honest dealing and strict adherence to the view that, for you to gain, those you deal with should gain as well."—Alan Greenspan, Economist and former Chairman of the Federal Reserve of the United States.

Dealers love to deal; it is their passion, their art, their work and for them…there is little to top it.

Literally

Dealer means "divider, distributor; agent, negotiator;" and in the sense of games, "a player who passes out the cards in a game" is from c.1600.

Dealer as a person; a retailer who deals in merchandise is noted from 1610s and the term in an illegal drug sense is recorded by 1920.

Deal is more to do with "a part or the share" and refers to the quantity or amount. So, this could apply to the terms or specifics of an agreement.

"Cutting a deal" is likely slang and also an idiom because it has its own peculiar, non-literal meaning of making an agreement.

History

While dealing has a long history, this will be a short section. Suffice to say that dealers and dealing have probably been around forever; an integral part of the way that people interact and function together. Deals and dealing are found in just about every human interaction from relationships, to families, to business, to government and globally.

Stories

A television story ...
'Secret Dealers' is a United Kingdom reality television show, where professional antique dealers are invited into people's homes to bid for items of interest. Three dealers bid in competition with each other and the owners then appraise the bids and decide what to sell.

At the end of each segment the show's presenter, Kate Bliss, gives the owners cash for the items that they agreed to sell. This is followed by a brief review of the dealer's success with on-selling the items and any profits realized.

Points to note:

- Dealers are generally interested in items that they can sell quickly and turn a profit.
- Dealers are aware of popular trends and recent sale prices of similar items.
- Dealers are efficient and visibly enjoy their work, and are generally knowledgeable, particularly in their specialty areas.
- Occasionally dealers will bid beyond the scope of making money, to add an item to their private collection.
- Most owners already know how they are going to spend the money, even before they receive a bid.
- Owners will often refuse a bid because it is less than what they paid, despite an independent expert's valuation confirming the dealer's bid as fair.
- Owners will place greater value on items with a personal or emotional connection e.g. "It belonged to my father" or "I knew it as a child."
- Owners sometimes offer items that they have no intention selling; just to get a valuation.
- Rarely, if ever, do owners accept all of the dealer's bids, to gain the maximum cash offered.

An antique story ...
While living on the Sunshine Coast in Queensland, I purchased several antique pieces from a dealer, Patsy Kimble. Patsy has a business in Buderim and often presents at antique fairs across the state with her associate Craig.

I found her at Pomona's annual antique fair and noticed that she had a beautiful sterling silver, Georgian bon bon dish with 3 exquisitely shaped legs. It was very pretty and I asked Patsy about the item. Her eyes lit up as she described the dish to me and clearly, she liked it too.

Two hundred and fifty dollars was printed on the price tag and I asked her if she was able to be flexible with that number. She looked down for a moment, probably running some numbers through her head, and then looked me in the eye and said, "You know, I was able to buy this for a good price and I'd like you to have it. I can go to one hundred and fifty. Is that okay?" In that moment, I knew I was with a true dealer.

Lets look at that:

- Patsy enjoyed the item with me; she liked it and that had probably been a factor in her buying the dish in the first place. At the same time she had no commitment to it; no emotional attachment.

- Having already assured her profit in the previous deal she was able and willing to bargain, and cleverly offered a substantial discount, which she knew would be hard for me to resist.

- Being generous with the deal, she left room for

me to profit, if I on-sold the piece. She made some money while allowing that future possibility for me too.

- She was gracious, in the sense that if I didn't buy that was fine and if I did then that was also fine. She allowed my choice without pushing her own viewpoint.

- When I paid and the item was snugly wrapped in tissue paper she said, "If ever you would like to sell this dish, please come and see me again." indicating that she still considered it valuable; desirable and that I was going home with a nice piece.

I have bought various items from Patsy Kimble and at different times she embodies all of the characters, employing them at her bidding and when they are required. She is a dealer.

A seminar story…
I'd like to introduce you to someone else that I know, his name is Gary Douglas and he is a dealer; in antiques and in other areas. This story is about one of the other areas.

Gary presents seminars; his business is called Access Consciousness and his work is making things move. People come to Gary's classes for many different reasons but what he invites everyone to, is change and transformation.

He is aware that people are stuck; stuck in their jobs, stuck in their relationships, stuck in their lives. He knows that they have been holding on tight, for as long as they can and that they are unaware they are stuck. He works with them using tools he has created, and teaches them how to use his tools.

He views "stuck" as energies and seeks to move or change the energies that people have used to create their stuck-points; the places they are locked in to; the places they are unaware of.

Gary uses all of the characters to manipulate and make deals. Often people will not give up their stuck-points unless it's a good deal. Gary is a dealer, he can make things move.

Dealer is not always about business or money; but it is always about movement, transformation and change. Gary's deals move people towards choices they did not know they had access to. He deals them a new hand and asks them to choose. He can make things move and he makes money. The people who are stuck pay him; the rewards are incredibly high and in ways you cannot imagine.

With every seminar and each new deal Gary makes; with each person who comes unstuck, he moves closer to his own target of greater awareness and consciousness in the world.

Taking Advantage

Dealers like to make deals and money; taking advantage of them requires skill and awareness. Dealers often have their own, private collections, hunt for treasure or invest and if you have something; an item that they want then they may pay you generously for it.

When a dealer desires an item for their private collection, for example, Collector can come to the fore very strongly. I recall a dealer mentioning to me they were interested in old sterling silver candlestick holders and had quite a few already. While hunting for treasure I found a pair, circa 1760, and put down a holding deposit. Later, I mentioned it to the dealer, suggesting that I might like to keep them for myself. I held off selling, they pursued me for the pieces, eventually we made a deal and I sold the pair. At this stage the price seemed irrelevant to them and I made a profit. The deal we made left headroom for their future profit too, if they chose to on-sell.

Be aware that while dealers are very capable of using all of the characters to advantage, there are times when they are influenced strongly by those very characters. When you notice this then *be a dealer* and make money, but don't make the mistake of stripping the cupboard bare; they will remember you and may be less likely to play next time.

Being Advantage

Dealers like to deal; their ability to "size-up" a deal i.e. grasp all of the parts and pieces; connect all of the players together and facilitate a deal can be remarkable.

Dealers are often multitalented and access the skills of collectors, treasure hunters, bargainers, speculators and investors as required. They are flexible and adapt easily as circumstances change. Dealers know when a deal is possible and what needs to be handled for it to progress.

Dealers can be dynamic sales people. I recall overhearing a conversation between someone enquiring about a college course and a dealer/salesman. The dealer simply asked questions until he had all of the person's concerns and skillfully provided solutions to each one; then he asked, "Is there anything else that would stop you from taking this course?" The enquirer came in that afternoon to sign up.

Dealers can be generous and in their enjoyment of what they love to do, they are a lot of fun.

Quiz

Use the following questions to review what you recall about this chapter:

1. What are five of the many capacities a dealer can have?

2. What is the job of a dealer (think log jams); what does it entail?

3. What two key elements make up the business that dealers are in?

4. What was Alan Greenspan's viewpoint?

5. In *Secret Dealers*, most owners have no idea what they will spend the money on. True or false?

6. When did Patsy Kimble make her profit, when selling me a silver dish?

7. What would you have to be aware of to take advantage of a dealer?

Self Reflection

In reading the previous sections you may have identified certain characteristics that you have. Use the following questions to access greater awareness and clarity in this area:

- Where are all of the places and spaces that you are dealing yourself the weakest hand?

- How many deals have you gathered together, hunted down, thought about endlessly, bargained dry or supported that have you stuck now?

- What deal will you not walk away from that is costing you more than you know?

- What limited number of talents and abilities have you decided you can handle that prevents you dealing yourself a winning hand every time?

- What deals are you working hard to keep alive that are already dead?

- How many deals have you squeezed so much juice out of that there is nothing left in them for you?

- Where are all the places you have been functioning in reverse by buying high and selling low?

- What dealer are you truly capable of being now?

Epilogue

Final Thoughts

If you are a treasure hunter, for example, and are good at finding treasure, then, if you'd like to make money you have to sell some treasure; you have to deal.

I love rummaging around secondhand stores, garage sales, bric-a-brac and the like. And wandering around the park with a metal detector is brilliant fun. I enjoy the hunt for treasure and often, find some great items. I do a bit of speculating too about how much money I could make, 'Should I keep it for a while or sell it now?' After a while another bright shiny treasure gets my attention and so my cupboards fill up. Eventually, I have a big clear out and throw things away or donate them to a charity shop. You may have noticed that there's not much money in that; except the money that I spent.

I still love rummaging around, but these days I can deal and make money. I get that now.

There's more though, and surprisingly it doesn't include money. I've stopped making treasure hunting *all* about money; treasure is not always precious metal, coins or jewels.

Near my home I've adopted a beach; actually a beautiful cove with a beach. A couple of times each week I go out and hunt for a different kind of treasure; rubbish. I pick up trash that is left by people or gets washed-up from the bay. It's funny, but since writing this book the energy; that joy of treasure hunting has expanded into many other areas of my life.

Finding a plastic bag hidden in amongst the rocks is a thrill, every time. And it gives me immense pleasure to know that the plastic bag I find is not going to end up in the stomach of one of our local sea turtles, and make it sick or kill it; or that a jagged piece of broken glass is not going to slice open the foot of a child playing on the beach. The payment is there, it's incredibly high and in ways I could not have imagined before Dealers.

Dealers are people that make things move; including trash. Dealers can change just about anything. What about you? What movement; what change are you truly capable of now?

Appendix

Additional, Bonus Material

There are two characteristics that require some explanation, though in themselves do not merit a full chapter. Gamblers and hoarders can be addictive or extreme traits that may occur with the other five characters.

For example, collectors may become addicted to collecting and hoard; speculators may gamble on their speculations.

The following offers explanation of these two intriguing rascals.

Stephen Outram

Gambling

Playing Risky Games

Gamble means to "play, jest, be merry" and, in itself, has little to do with winning, losing, betting or money.

When you watch young children playing, you will observe that there is little there about someone winning. They play with the simplest of things and effortlessly create their games as an ongoing, fun adventure. Without intervention, children's games rarely end but transform into new activities. Their games generally end when parents get involved, otherwise children play; they gamble.

> "I engage students in my class in the game of Yahtzee, to teach certain aspects of language. They are never interested in adding up the score at the end; they enjoy the activity of playing,"— Simone Phillips, Dip. Teaching, Languages

Gambling has a bad reputation these days and so it's not socially acceptable to say, "Wow! Look at my children. They are having such fun gambling." How did we get from play, jest and be merry, to *bad*? More on that later.

Young animals, take puppies for example, eat, sleep and play. One moment puppies are in an energetic tussle and the next they have fallen asleep on top of each other. In the tussle it may seem like they are competing, but wrestling and biting is an important part of how they learn to become dogs.

> "Play fighting is an essential part of early canine development. Mock brawls are an instinctual urge in puppies. It helps them learn to control the strength of their bite and how to socialize with other dogs."— Quentin Coleman, for The Daily Puppy

Children and puppies gambling seems quite natural, instinctive and fun; so how does gambling become a problem?

> "…gambling can be highly destructive – ruining lives and destroying families."—Problem Gambling, Australian Government

Many of you will know the popular and long-lived board game Monopoly, played and enjoyed by children and adults worldwide. While Monopoly did promote competition—winning and losing— amongst players, in recent times something else has been added to the game; betting or wagering. Today, Monopoly themed betting games are featured in slot machines, quizzes, bingo, etc. and can be played online for *real* money. And here we begin to see how gambling has become misidentified as a problem.

> "…studies show that some children do start gambling very young – as young as 10. The majority of them have gambled by the age of 15."—*Gamblers and Teenagers*, Raising Children Network

Gambling is just playing, but when competition is added to it then the elements of winning and losing can become significant. Competition is introduced by having a prize, for example, a cup, ribbon or certificate; and in addition, the rules of the game. A competition's rules work to determine the conditions of play and an end point, as play stops with the conclusion of a winner.

A competition that features a winner is susceptible to a powerful outside influence, that of people making bets on who or what will be the winner. And right there, like a mosquito or a tick, you find a parasite that sucks the play out of gambling and transforms how it is perceived. By association, it seems that gambling has been judged harshly as something that it's not, making it a problem.

There is much that has been written about gambling and betting; it is the subject of thousands of publications. In relation to Dealers and the other characters described in this book, please note that when you add competition and associated betting to gambling, then something different must emerge.

When the invention of "auction," with its inherent competition, winner and losers; is added to the world of our friend Bargainer, it can have a highly manipulative effect. And if a third party organization offered betting on the outcomes of auctions, then auctions and their bidders may also be perceived as problems.

Speculators, who create extreme scenarios in their minds, may bet on the outcomes they imagine will make them rich. This action has created speculation being perceived as a high risk activity, when it's not.

Dealers who bet on the *chance* of making money on a deal will likely lose; treasure hunters who take on wagers relating to the success of their hunt and collectors banking on hope, may all fall victim to their lack of awareness around something that turns their enjoyable game into to a profitless nightmare.

You can bet upon just about anything these days; two flies running up a wall can be enough to entice people to bet or wager an outcome. This is not gambling, though the two flies playing on the wall may be. Make sure that you do not confuse gambling and betting as these two are quite different. It may cost you if you do, and invariably does.

If you have judged gambling as bad or made it a problem, then you may never enjoy playing your favorite game.

Stephen Outram

Hoarding

Hidden Treasure

Throughout history there have been many times when people have concealed their valuables and created hidden treasure.

Hoarding has gotten a poor reputation recently, thanks to reality television shows such as *Hoarders*, featuring people who have filled their homes to the point of bursting, with all manner of worthless junk. More on that later.

History reveals that people hoard when their livelihood, homes or very lives are threatened. During wars or invasions, when people are forced to abandon their countries and flee to safer lands, they will often bury or conceal wealth that they are unable to take with them in the hope of returning and reclaiming it, sometime in the future.

> " Mr Martin Sulzbacher, a German Jew, had fled Nazi Germany with his wealth and settled in London in 1938…his family, fearing an imminent German invasion of Britain, buried his coins in the back garden of their Hackney property. Tragically, they perished in the Blitz"—Hackney Hoard, Ian Richardson, British Museum

Hoard means "treasure, valuable stock or store" and "to cover or conceal;" literally hidden treasure.

Hoards have been found in a variety of locations from suburban homes to farmer's fields, temples and battle sites of military campaigns.

"…the Grouville Hoard is exceptional. In the early 1980s, acting on a rumor that a farmer had once found silver coins on his land, two metal detector fans began a search for treasure. They spent the next 30 years searching off and on until finally, in 2012, their persistence paid off when they discovered an estimated 70,000 Iron Age and Roman silver and gold coins on the eastern edge of the island of Jersey."—Michael Leach, from *10 Amazing Treasure Hoards Found in Recent Years*

The action of hoarding valuables, though more dramatized when treasure hunters find fabulous ancient hoards, is done widely today as people hoard their money in banks; hiding it from view and hopefully, in safety. In fact, the digital age has allowed money to become virtual and displayed as pixels on a computer monitor; protected by passwords and sophisticated encryption. The widespread use of credit cards conceals that money has been transacted. Those who do not trust banks, may resort to hiding money under the mattress of their bed, the freezer compartment of their refrigerator or other novel and unusual places.

Hoarding is alive and well and whatever it is that people value, they will go to extraordinary lengths to conceal and protect it; sometimes to their disadvantage:

> "A man accidentally threw $50,000 worth of gold in the bin… he had accidentally thrown out the jewellery and gold bars after earlier splitting them into three different garbage bags to fool any would-be thieves."—Courier Mail, 2013, Queensland, Australia

Compulsive hoarding has been categorized as a disorder related to Obsessive Compulsive Disorder (OCD). Dr. Eric Hollander notes that a "…study found that people with hoarding disorder took much longer to make decisions about discarding their possessions and felt more sadness and anxiety about these choices … people feel this sense of discomfort if they feel like they may be giving away something that they could use in future."

The USA documentary TV series *Hoarders* depicted the real-life struggles and treatment of people who suffer from compulsive hoarding. The show's cameras filmed people's homes where just about every room was filled with all manner of relatively valueless stuff, for example, stacks of old newspapers.

My sense of this "compulsive" activity is that it is not hoarding but more related to consumption (a wasting disease), where certain people have a phobia that there is not enough, there will never be enough and everything must be kept and not wasted; perhaps for an imagined and empty future.

In relationship to our characters, hoarding may be seen as something connected strongly with Collectors, perhaps an extreme collecting; it is not. Hoarding is more related to storing or hiding valuables, particularly in times of trouble, rather than the ancient and long-lived profession of Tax Collector, for example. Treasure Hunters most certainly search for and hope to find hoards.

In times of trouble, hoarding makes sense i.e. hide your gold away safely and come back later when the dust has settled. And in 2014 and beyond, with governments being very keen to extract as much money from the population as possible, hoarding may be an option that some people will choose.

> "If government is broke and they are raising taxes on everything possible, what would you do? When people fear government and banks, they spend less and hoard more. Follow the money if you want the truth."—Martin Armstrong, from *Follow the Money*, May 2014

And if you do choose to hoard, then make sure you and yours are the ones who find it in the future!

Stephen Outram

About The Author

Biography

Stephen Outram has a background of some 18 years in architecture, and since 1997 has worked as a graphic artist, website developer and Internet consultant. More recently he has written several books, spoken and presented seminars on a number of topics, including the "Making Money with Change" series,

Educated in Queensland, Australia, Stephen studied at Brisbane's University of Technology in the 1970s. He returned to study in 1995 at Dundee University, Scotland, achieving a Master of Science degree in Computing.

His family emigrated to Australia, from the United Kingdom in 1965, originally landing in Freemantle, Western Australia and spending 5 years in the northerly town of Port Hedland. In 1970 the family drove across the country from west to east and settled in Queensland's Gold Coast, where his parents and sister still reside.

Stephen enjoys a diverse and wide range of projects including work, writing, music and song writing, boats and some sport. He is active with Surfrider Foundation Australia and is interested in sustainable and flourishing coastlines and waterways, free of plastics and pollution.

For more information, visit the website:

stephenoutram.com

Other Books

By Stephen Outram

Public Speaking: Beyond Fear

Public Speaking: Beyond Fear is designed for people who experience difficulty with public speaking and performance. It will also benefit people who think they have it all handled.

The ideas, concepts and tools contained in this book may catapult you to levels of freedom and ease with public speaking that you've never had before.

- Harness! The power of fear
- Symptoms. Anxiety is your best friend
- Explore! The weird, *hidden issues* that you can change
- Begin functioning beyond normal
- Fight Flight! Working *with* your body
- Why amateurs never get paid

What if your journey with public speaking was really an adventure, unfolding before you with each new choice you make?

Advanced Speaking Concepts

Advanced Speaking Concepts is written for people who are seeking to create something greater and something different with public speaking. It will also benefit people who are beginning; the new generation of speakers.

This book contains ideas and concepts to assist you going beyond all of the old, worn public speaking techniques that everyone else uses to be competent, average and safe.

- Exposed! The myth that public speaking is the No.1 fear.
- The weird and hidden issues that are holding you back.
- Nerves! Why you need them to perform better.
- Applause. A beginning, not the end.
- Manipulation! Using it to advantage.

What if your journey with public speaking was really an adventure unfolding before you with each new choice you make?

More information at stephenoutram.com

Notes

Stephen Outram

www.ingramcontent.com/pod-product-compliance
Lightning Source LLC
Chambersburg PA
CBHW020013050426
42450CB00005B/454